Bilingual WORDS
SCHOOL • ENGLISH – SPANISH
1000
ESCUELA • INGLÉS – ESPAÑOL
PALABRAS bilingües

Written by Gill Budgell
Senior Editor Dawn Sirett
Senior Designer Rachael Parfitt Hunt
Designers Kanika Kalra, Mansi Dwivedi, Rhys Thomas, Sif Nørskov
US Editor Jane Perlmutter
US Senior Editor Shannon Beatty
Additional editorial work Robin Moul
Additional illustrations Rhys Thomas, Mohd Zishan
DTP Designers Dheeraj Singh, Syed Md Farhan
Picture Researcher Rituraj Singh
Jacket Designer Sif Nørskov
Jacket Coordinator Elin Woosnam
Production Editor Becky Fallowfield
Production Controller John Casey
Managing Editor Penny Smith
Delhi Creative Head Malavika Talukder
Art Director Mabel Chan
Publisher Francesca Young
Publishing Director Sarah Larter

Bilingual edition
Editorial Services Tinta Simpàtica
Translation Anna Nualart
Project Coordination Marina Alcione
Editorial Direction Elsa Vivente

First American Edition, 2024
Published in the United States by DK Publishing,
a division of Penguin Random House LLC
1745 Broadway, 20th Floor, New York, NY 10019

Original title: *1000 More Words*
First bilingual edition: 2024
Copyright © 2024 Dorling Kindersley Limited
© Spanish translation 2024 Dorling Kindersley Limited

ISBN: 978-0-5938-4820-3

DK books are available at special discounts when purchased in bulk
for sales promotions, premiums, fund-raising, or educational use.
For details, contact: DK Publishing Special Markets,
1745 Broadway, 20th Floor, New York, NY 10019
SpecialSales@dk.com

Printed and bound in China

www.dkespañol.com

Bilingual WORDS
SCHOOL • ENGLISH – SPANISH

1000

ESCUELA • INGLÉS – ESPAÑOL
PALABRAS bilingües

Gill Budgell

DK

A note for parents and carers about language for learning
Nota para padres y cuidadores sobre el lenguaje para el aprendizaje

This bilingual book focuses on more of the vocabulary young children need to learn both English and Spanish, whether in school or in their everyday lives.

As children learn, they need to read, write, and spell words that relate to a variety of topics and subjects. They need to be able to listen and speak with confidence too.

1000 Words: School features vocabulary that will help children learn about literacy skills, mathematics, science, the arts, PE, and sports, as well as some more challenging vocabulary about geography and history. There are also words about technology, since increasingly the language of technology is embedded in every aspect of our learning. We talk about digital communication, digital devices, as well as ways to create and present information in a more data-led world.

A broad vocabulary can help children to access their education more easily with a sense of curiosity and engagement. It enables them to name, describe, explain, and sort their learning into categories, as well as to see overlaps between different areas of learning.

Spending time with children to talk about the words and pictures representing different areas of learning within this book will ensure that children consolidate what they know and extend their knowledge and understanding. This book is a great place to begin sharing words in English and Spanish while enjoying discussions with your child, but remember to continue the conversations in your day-to-day life too.

Gill Budgell
Early years and primary language consultant, trainer, and author

Este libro bilingüe se centra en el vocabulario que los más pequeños necesitan para aprender el inglés y el español, tanto en la escuela como en su vida diaria.

A medida que aprenden, los niños deben leer, escribir y deletrear palabras relacionadas con diversos temas y materias. También deben poder escuchar y hablar con confianza.

1000 Palabras: Escuela presenta vocabulario que les ayudará a aprender sobre las habilidades de lectura y escritura, matemáticas, ciencias, artes, educación física y deportes, así como otro vocabulario más complejo sobre geografía e historia. También se incluyen palabras sobre tecnología, porque el lenguaje tecnológico está cada vez más presente en todos los aspectos del aprendizaje. Se habla de comunicación digital, de dispositivos digitales y de formas de crear y presentar la información en un mundo cada vez más basado en los datos.

Un vocabulario amplio ayuda a los niños en su educación con una mayor curiosidad e implicación. Les permite nombrar, describir, explicar y clasificar en categorías aquello que aprenden, y también observar cómo se solapan las distintas áreas del aprendizaje.

Dedicar tiempo a hablar con los niños sobre las palabras y los dibujos de las distintas áreas garantiza que consoliden lo que saben y amplíen su comprensión y conocimientos. Este libro es un buen punto de partida para compartir palabras en inglés y en español y disfrutar de la conversación con ellos, pero es importante seguir conversando también en la vida cotidiana.

Gill Budgell
Consultora, formadora y autora sobre el lenguaje de las etapas inicial y de primaria

Contents
Contenidos

Let's communicate
Comuniquémonos

When we communicate we share information, stories, feelings, or ideas. There are many ways to do this, including speaking, signing, writing, or dancing. Here are words we use for these things.

Cuando nos comunicamos, compartimos información, historias, sentimientos o ideas. Hay muchas formas de hacerlo, como hablar, cantar, escribir o bailar. Aquí tienes algunas palabras que usamos para estas cosas.

Communication
Comunicación

speak
hablar

discuss
conversar

listen
escuchar

sign
señalar

present
presentar

ask
preguntar

join in
participar

dance
bailar

act
actuar

paint
pintar

Learning to read
Aprender a leer

a b c d e
f g h i j k
l m n ñ o
p q r s t u
v w x y z

letters
letras

Braille
braille

picture
foto

words
palabras

This is my friend.
Este es mi amigo
Esta es mi amiga

sentence
frase

book
libro

Learning to write
Aprender a escribir

writing guidelines
pautas de escritura

copying and tracing
copiar y calcar

hello
hola
(English)
(inglés)

left to right
de izquierda a derecha

مرحبا

right to left
de derecha a izquierda

("hello" in Arabic)
("hola" en árabe)

新年快乐

top to bottom
de arriba abajo

("Happy New Year" in Chinese)
("Feliz año nuevo" en chino)

Languages are written left to right, right to left, or sometimes top to bottom.
Las lenguas se escriben de izquierda a derecha, de derecha a izquierda o, a veces, de arriba abajo.

Feelings
Sentimientos

amazed
asombrada

satisfied
contento

Try making the faces for these feelings.

Intenta hacer las caras de estos sentimientos.

brave
osada

upset
decepcionado

puzzled
confundido

shy
tímida

excited
emocionada

frustrated
frustrado

7

Reading and writing
Leer y escribir

Why do we read and write? Reading helps us learn and gives us pleasure. Writing helps us communicate and record our communications. Here are words we use when we read and write.

¿Por qué leemos y escribimos? Leer nos ayuda a aprender y es una fuente de placer. Escribir nos ayuda a comunicar y dejar constancia de nuestras comunicaciones. Aquí tienes algunas palabras que usamos cuando leemos y escribimos.

Different types of reading
Distintos tipos de lectura

independent
en solitario

paired
en pareja

shared
compartida

guided
guiada

What books do you like to read?
¿Qué libros te gusta leer?

Fiction
Ficción

stories
cuentos

El mundo del dragón — DRAGON WORLD

¡Ataque pirata!

PIRATE ATTACK!

fantasy
fantasía

adventure
aventuras

picture book
libro ilustrado

chapter book
libro en capítulos

Nonfiction
No ficción

information
información

dictionary
diccionario

report
reportaje

NEWS NOTICIAS

How to make muffins
Cómo hacer magdalenas

newspaper
periódico

instructions
instrucciones

Reading everywhere!
¡Leer en todas partes!

OPEN ABIERTO

sign
cartel

JAM MERMELADA

label
etiqueta

board game
juego de tablero

How to play
Cómo se juega

instructions
instrucciones

Braille is used by people who are blind or have low vision.
El braille lo utilizan las personas ciegas o que tienen poca visión.

raised dots that you feel
puntos en relieve que se notan

Let's write!
¡Vamos a escribir!

right-handed
diestra

left-handed
zurdo

pencil
lápiz

brush
pincel

paper
papel

tablet
tableta

pen
bolígrafo

tablet stylus
estilete de tableta

lined paper
papel pautado

sharpener
sacapuntas

eraser
goma

ruler
regla

Writing tools, materials, and equipment
Útiles de escritura, materiales y equipamiento

Reasons to write
Razones para escribir

Books to read
Libros para leer

list
lista

Happy birthday!
¡Feliz cumpleaños!

card
tarjeta

Remember to brush your teeth!
¡Acuérdate de lavarte los dientes!

note
nota

Please come to my party.
Por favor, ven a mi fiesta.

invitation
invitación

Dear friend,
Querido amigo,

letter
carta

Adding up
Sumar

Add up the numbers on the sails.
Write the total on the boats.
Suma los números de las velas.
Escribe el total en los barcos.

homework
deberes

Preparing to write
Prepararse para escribir

? ?

thinking
pensar

?

ideas
ideas

Kitten gets stuck!
¡El gatito no sabe bajar!

planning
planificar

9

Languages of the world
Lenguas del mundo

The languages we speak are part of who we are. Let's find out how to write and pronounce "hello" in ten of the most widely spoken languages in the world.

Las lenguas que hablamos son una parte de lo que somos. Descubramos cómo se escribe y pronuncia "hola" en diez de los idiomas más hablados del mundo.

Chinese
chino

你好

Chinese script
caligrafía china

Say "nee-how."
Di "ni-hao".

Russian
ruso

привет

Cyrillic script
alfabeto cirílico

Say "pri-vyet."
Di "pri-viet".

Japanese
japonés

こんにちは

hiragana script
escritura hiragana

Say "kon-nee-chee-wah."
Di "kon-ni-chi-ua".

Arabic
árabe

مرحبا

Arabic abjad script
alfabeto árabe abyad

Say "mar-haba."
Di "mar-haba".

Hindi
hindi

नमस्ते

Devanagari script
escritura devanagari

Say "nuh-must-ay"
Di "na-mas-te".

Bengali
bengalí

হ্যালো

Bengali script
escritura bengalí

Say "hel-o."
Di "hel-o".

Korean
coreano

안녕하세요

Hangul script
alfabeto hangul

Say "ann-yong-ha-sey-oh."
Di "an-nyeong-ja-se-yo".

English
inglés

Hello

Latin script
alfabeto latino

Say "hel-low."
Di "hel-lou".

Spanish
castellano

Hola

Latin script
alfabeto latino

Say "oh-la."
Di "o-la".

Portuguese
portugués

Olá

accent
acento

Latin script
alfabeto latino

Say "oh-la."
Di "o-la".

What languages do you speak?
¿Qué lenguas hablas?

"Hello" in sign language
"Hola" en lengua de señas

Can you sign hello?
¿Sabes decir hola con señas?

"Hello" in Braille
(a written code for languages)

— raised dots
puntos en relieve

"Hola" en braille
(código escrito para las lenguas)

Whistling language for long-distance communication
Lenguaje silbado para comunicarse a mucha distancia

Emojis
emojis

Computer code (programming language)
Código informático (lenguaje de programación)

01000001   01000010   01000011

A   B   C

binary number system
sistema numérico binario

Ancient languages
Lenguas antiguas

A   B   C   D   E

Sumerian
(from an area that is modern-day Iraq)
sumerio
(de la zona del actual Irak)

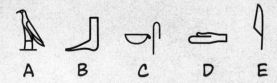

A   B   C   D   E

Egyptian hieroglyphs
jeroglíficos egipcios

Naming things
Nombrar cosas

Words that name places, people, objects, animals, and ideas are called nouns.

Las palabras que nombran lugares, personas, objetos, animales e ideas se llaman sustantivos.

At a hospital, we might use these nouns.

En un hospital podríamos utilizar estos sustantivos.

Places
Lugares

reception
recepción

waiting room
sala de espera

consulting room
consulta

dispensary
dispensario

emergency room
servicio de urgencias

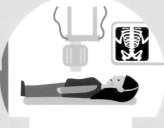

x-ray room
sala de rayos X

operating room
quirófano

ward
pabellón

People
Personas

line
cola

nurse
enfermero

medical receptionist
recepcionista médica

patient
paciente

doctor
doctor

paramedic
enfermera

Objects
Objetos

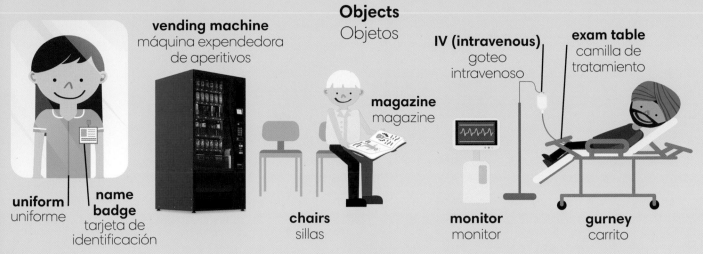

uniform
uniforme

name badge
tarjeta de identificación

vending machine
máquina expendedora de aperitivos

chairs
sillas

magazine
magazine

IV (intravenous)
goteo intravenoso

exam table
camilla de tratamiento

monitor
monitor

gurney
carrito

Ideas
Ideas

healthy eating
alimentación saludable

thought
pensamiento

strength
fortaleza

success
éxito

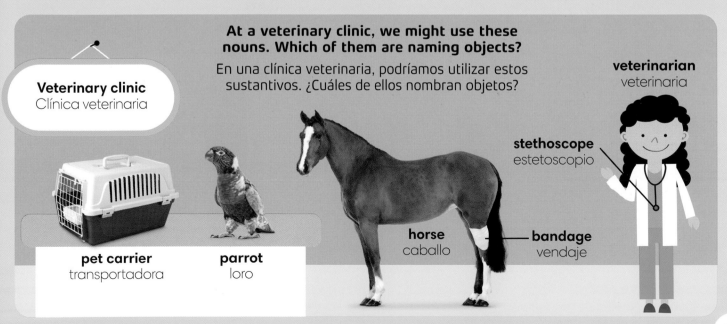

At a veterinary clinic, we might use these nouns. Which of them are naming objects?

En una clínica veterinaria, podríamos utilizar estos sustantivos. ¿Cuáles de ellos nombran objetos?

Veterinary clinic
Clínica veterinaria

veterinarian
veterinaria

stethoscope
estetoscopio

pet carrier
transportadora

parrot
loro

horse
caballo

bandage
vendaje

Describing things
Describir cosas

Words that describe people, places, objects, animals, and ideas are called adjectives. Choose an adjective that describes you!

Las palabras que describen personas, lugares, objetos, animales e ideas se llaman adjetivos. ¡Elige un adjetivo que te describa!

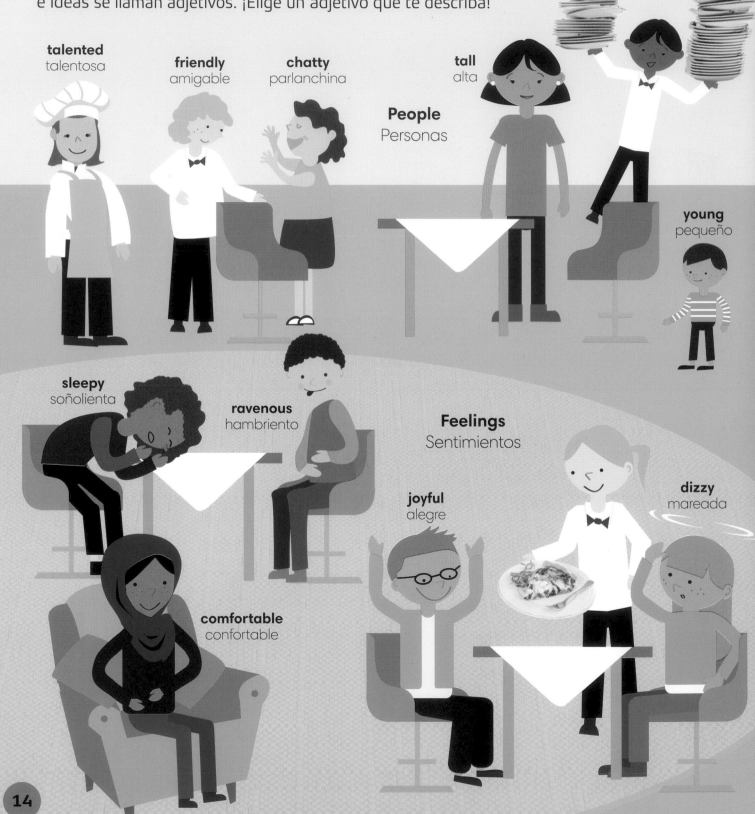

skillful
habilidoso

talented
talentosa

friendly
amigable

chatty
parlanchina

tall
alta

People
Personas

young
pequeño

sleepy
soñolienta

ravenous
hambriento

Feelings
Sentimientos

comfortable
confortable

joyful
alegre

dizzy
mareada

Size and volume
Tamaño y volumen

supersized — extragrande

enormous — enorme

tiny — minúsculo

overflowing — rebosante

yummy — delicioso

juicy — jugoso

fruity — afrutado

chilled — helado

steady — lento

quickly — ágil

Food
Comida

sugary — azucarado

fresh — fresco

spicy — picante

chocolatey — achocolatado

Movement
Movimiento

speedy — rápida

smelly — apestoso

sparkling — espumoso

scorching — ardiente

beige — beige

vibrant — vibrante

Color
Color

vivid — vivo

What's going on?
¿Qué ocurre?

Some words describe what people or things are doing, or what people are thinking or feeling. These words are called verbs.

Algunas palabras describen lo que hacen las personas o las cosas, o lo que las personas piensan o sienten. Estas palabras se llaman verbos.

Which of these things would you like to do?
¿Cuáles de estas cosas te gustaría hacer?

prepare
preparar

reach
alcanzar

Stretch!
¡Estira!

What would you like?
¿Qué te apetece?

frown
fruncir el ceño

decide
decidir

ask
preguntar

dislike
no gustar

Stop!
¡Para!

forget
olvidar

notice
avisar

lick
lamer

skip
saltar

pull
tirar

block
parar

kick
patear

sniff
oler

16

climb up
trepar

ascend
subir

wait
esperar

descend
bajar

zoom down
deslizarse

hear
oír

feel
notar

admire
admirar

1, 2, 3…
1, 2, 3…

count
contar

hide
esconderse

Catch!
¡Agárralo!

sprint
correr

tiptoe
ir de
puntitas

whistle
silbar

giggle
reír

hug
abrazar

relax
descansar

yell
gritar

frighten
asustar

17

Adding detail
Añadir detalles

We can add detail to verbs by using words that say how, when, where, how often, and how much a thing happens. These words are called adverbs.

Podemos añadir detalles a los verbos utilizando palabras que digan cómo, cuándo, dónde, con qué frecuencia y cuánto ocurre algo. Estas palabras se llaman adverbios.

happily
felizmente

gracefully
elegantemente

loudly
ruidosamente

speedily
rápidamente

proudly
orgullosamente

angrily
con enfado

weakly
débilmente

bravely
valientemente

curiously
con curiosidad

How is the explorer exploring?
¿Cómo explora el explorador?

today
hoy

soon
pronto

now
ahora

tomorrow
mañana

When should the explorer go exploring?
¿Cuándo debe salir a explorar la exploradora?

on
en

up
arriba

down
abajo

around
alrededor

behind
detrás

above
encima

between
entre

near
cerca

opposite
frente

below
debajo

Where is the beetle climbing? Where is the beetle positioned?
¿Por dónde trepa el escarabajo? ¿Dónde está situado el escarabajo?

hourly
cada hora

yearly
anualmente

Calendar
Calendario

frequently
frecuentemente

little
poco

lots
mucho

sometimes
a veces

**How often and how much
do the birds sing?**
¿Con qué frecuencia y cuánto cantan los pájaros?

How often do the frogs eat?
¿Con qué frecuencia
comen las ranas?

19

All about numbers
Todo sobre los números

Here are words that help us play counting games and learn about numbers.

He aquí palabras que nos ayudan a contar cuando jugamos y a aprender los números.

winner
ganador

end
final

Playing with numbers
Jugar con números

board game
juego de mesa

roll
tirar

dice
dados

start
inicio

Types of numbers
Tipos de números

2, 4, 6, 8, 10
even numbers
números pares

1, 3, 5, 7, 9
odd numbers
números impares

13, 14, 15, 16, 17, 18, 19
teen numbers
números que en inglés terminan en "teen"

Counting
Counting

5, 10, 15, 20, 25
in fives
de cinco en cinco

10, 20, 30, 40, 50
in tens
por decenas

Place value
Valor posicional

3
3 ones
3 unidades

30
3 tens
3 decenas

300
3 hundreds
3 centenas

partition
partición

63

6 tens
6 decenas

3 ones
3 unidades

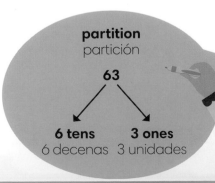

Ordinals
Ordinales

sixth sexto
fifth quinta
fourth cuarto
third tercera
second segundo
first primera

What are the missing numbers?
¿Cuáles son los números que faltan?

_____ ← 20
before
anterior

11 _____ 13
between
entre

17 → _____
after
posterior

Order these numbers from lowest to highest.
Ordena estos números del más bajo al más alto.

27   25   26

Number bonds
Enlaces numéricos

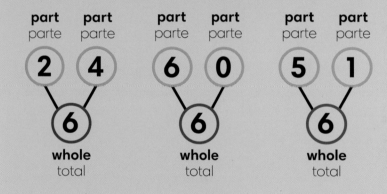

part parte **part** parte
(2) (4)
(6)
whole total

part parte **part** parte
(6) (0)
(6)
whole total

part parte **part** parte
(5) (1)
(6)
whole total

Addition
Suma

3 + 2 = 5

Subtraction
Resta

3 - 2 = 1

Shapes and space
Formas y espacio

Let's learn some shape names and some words about position and direction.

Aprendamos el nombre de algunas formas y algunas palabras sobre la posición y la dirección.

2D shape
Forma 2-D

flat
plano

square
cuadrado

4 corners
4 ángulos

4 sides
4 lados

Lines of symmetry for a square
Líneas de simetría de un cuadrado

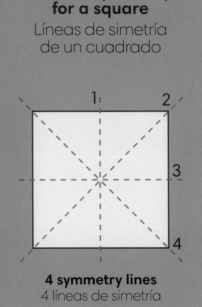

1   2

3

4

4 symmetry lines
4 líneas de simetría

3D shapes
Formas 3-D

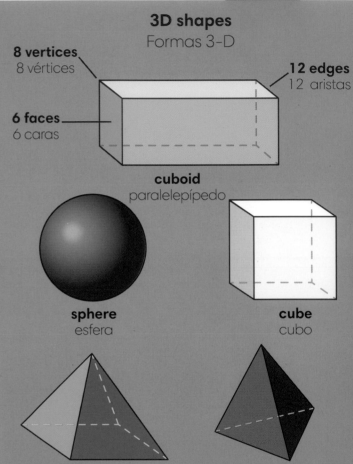

8 vertices
8 vértices

12 edges
12 aristas

6 faces
6 caras

cuboid
paralelepípedo

sphere
esfera

cube
cubo

square-based pyramid
pirámide de base cuadrada

triangular-based pyramid
pirámide de base triangular

cone
cono

triangular prism
prisma triangular

cylinder
cilindro

Polygons (2D shapes with 3 or more straight sides)
Polígonos (formas 2-D con 3 o más lados rectos)

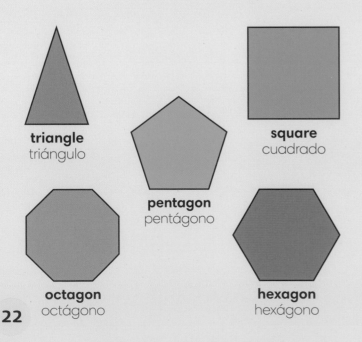

triangle
triángulo

pentagon
pentágono

square
cuadrado

octagon
octágono

hexagon
hexágono

Can you see any of these shapes near you?

¿Ves alguna de estas formas cerca de ti?

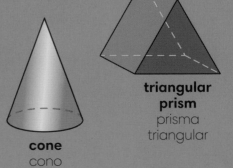

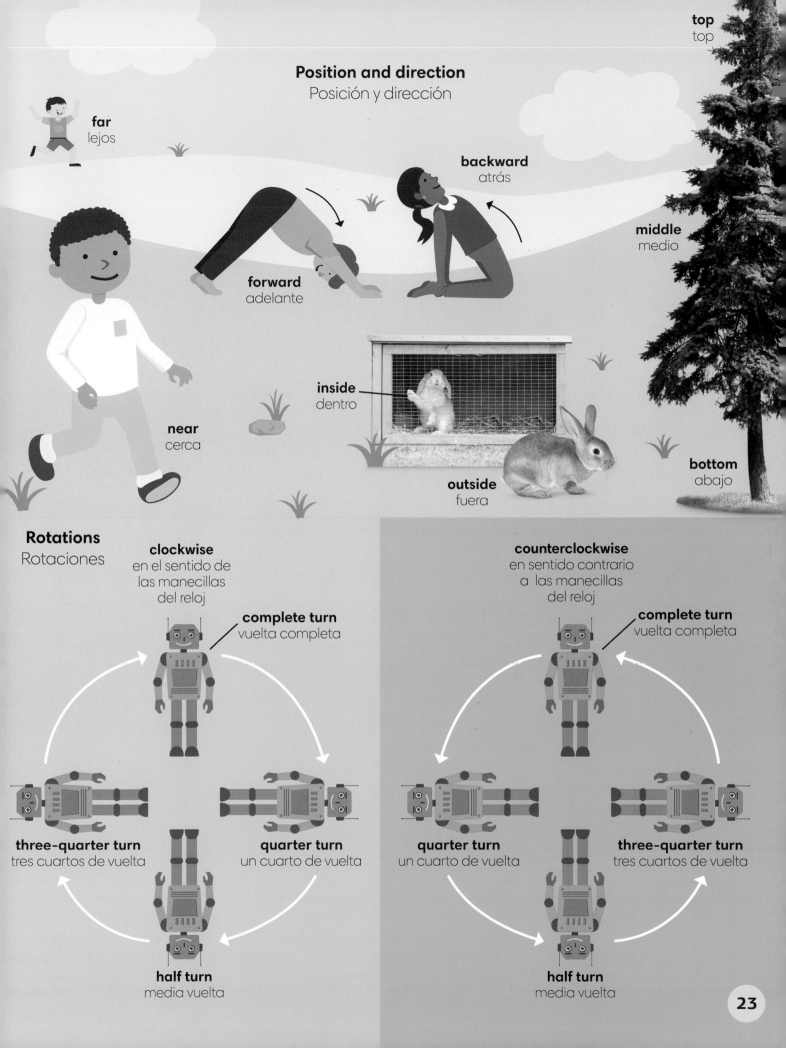

Position and direction
Posición y dirección

far
lejos

backward
atrás

middle
medio

forward
adelante

inside
dentro

near
cerca

outside
fuera

bottom
abajo

Rotations
Rotaciones

clockwise
en el sentido de
las manecillas
del reloj

counterclockwise
en sentido contrario
a las manecillas
del reloj

complete turn
vuelta completa

complete turn
vuelta completa

three-quarter turn
tres cuartos de vuelta

quarter turn
un cuarto de vuelta

quarter turn
un cuarto de vuelta

three-quarter turn
tres cuartos de vuelta

half turn
media vuelta

half turn
media vuelta

23

Talking about science
Hablar de ciencia

Here are some words we use when we are working together in science.

Estas son algunas palabras que usamos cuando colaboramos en las ciencias.

Can you think of some more equipment that you might use in a science lesson?

¿Se te ocurren más instrumentos que podrías utilizar en una clase de ciencias?

Let's be scientists
Seamos científicos

notice
ver

observe
observar

sort
ordenar

classify
clasificar

Some things we might use
Algunas cosas que podríamos utilizar

water
agua

food coloring
colorante alimentario

measuring spoons
cucharas de medida

microscope
microscopio

scale
balanza

stopwatch
cronómetro

funnel
embudo

magnet
imán

containers
contenedores

safety goggles
lentes de seguridad

ask questions
hacerse preguntas

compare
comparar

contrast
contrastar

gather data
obtener datos

Let's experiment
Experimentemos

prepare
preparar

fill
llenar

add
añadir

stir
agitar

help
ayudar

pour
verter

make
hacer

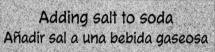

Adding salt to soda
Añadir sal a una bebida gaseosa

describe
describir

The drink fizzes and rises up!
¡La bebida burbujea y sube!

note sounds and smells
observar sonidos y olores

record results
anota los resultados

Describing materials
Describir materiales

Let's learn some words to help us describe everyday materials.

Aprendamos algunas palabras para describir los materiales cotidianos.

Natural materials
Materiales naturales

wool
lana

leather
piel

rubber
caucho

wood
madera

stones
piedras

rocks
rocas

clay
arcilla

glass
vidrio

steel
acero

plastic
papel

synthetic fabric
synthetic fabric

paper
papel

Manufactured materials
Materiales manufacturados

Can you think of two more things that are made of steel?
¿Se te ocurren dos cosas más que estén hechas de acero?

Opposites
Opuestos

transparent
transparente

opaque
opaco

shiny
brillante

dull
mate

hard
duro

soft
blando

stretchy
elástico

rigid
rígido

waterproof
impermeable

not waterproof
permeable

 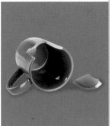

tough
resistente

brittle
frágil

absorbent
absorbente

not absorbent
no absorbente

heavy
pesado

light
ligero

fluffy
suave

spiky
espinoso

rough   **bumpy**
áspero   irregular

smooth
liso

bendable   **flexible**
curvado   flexible

stiff
rígido

All about art
Todo sobre el arte

Here are words about art and the names of some tools we use to make different kinds of art. Think of a picture you would like to create. What tool would you use to create it?

Aquí tienes palabras sobre arte y los nombres de algunas herramientas que usamos para hacer distintos tipos de arte. Piensa en un dibujo que te gustaría hacer. ¿Qué herramienta utilizarías para crearlo?

Mark making
Impresión de marcas

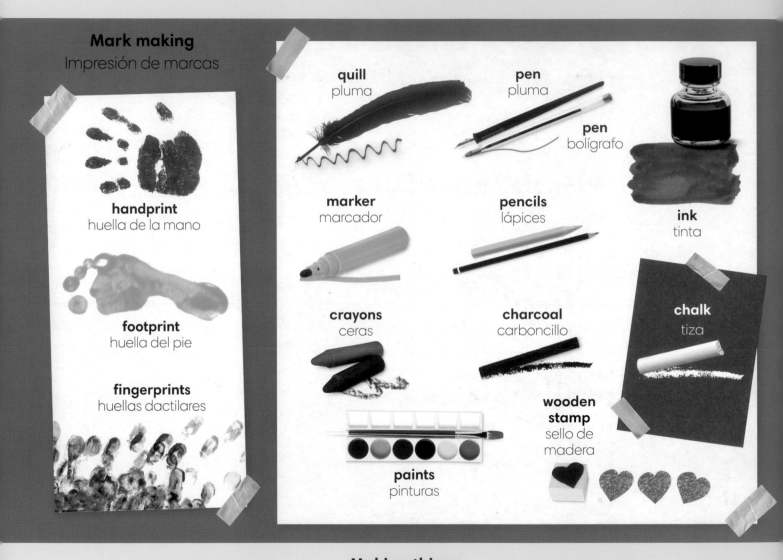

quill
pluma

pen
pluma

pen
bolígrafo

handprint
huella de la mano

marker
marcador

pencils
lápices

ink
tinta

footprint
huella del pie

crayons
ceras

charcoal
carboncillo

chalk
tiza

fingerprints
huellas dactilares

wooden stamp
sello de madera

paints
pinturas

Making things
Hacer cosas

sculpture
escultura

painting
pintura

collage
collage

architecture
arquitectura

pottery
cerámica

Digital art
Arte digital

photography
fotografía

camera
cámara

zoom lens
objetivo con zoom

close-up
primer plano

long shot
vista general

animation
animación

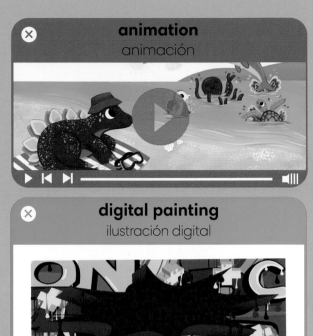

digital painting
ilustración digital

Colors
Colores

primary colors
colores primarios

mixing colors
mezclar colores

Tones
Tonos

tint
tinta

shadow
sombra

shade
sombreado

highlight
destacado

lighter colors
colores más claros

darker colors
colores más oscuros

29

Lines and patterns
Líneas y patrones

These words help us to describe patterns and designs. What patterns do you like?

Estas palabras nos ayudan a describir patrones y diseños. ¿Qué patrones te gustan?

If you were decorating a T-shirt with lines, which of the lines below would you choose?

Si tuvieras que decorar una camiseta con líneas, ¿cuál de estas líneas elegirías?

straight
rectas

horizontal
horizontales

vertical
verticales

diagonal
diagonales

parallel
paralelas

perpendicular
perpendiculares

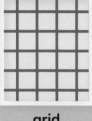

grid
cuadrícula

x's
cruces

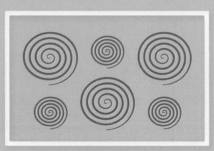

spirals
espirales

crosshatch
trama cruzada

smudged
emborronadas

waves
onduladas

dashes
discontinuas

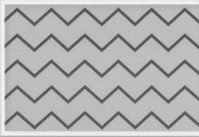

zigzag
zigzag

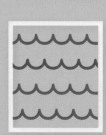

scalloped
festoneadas

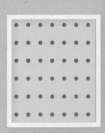

dotted
de puntos

loops
bucles

connected horizontal and vertical
horizontales y verticales unidas

Lines
Líneas

bouncy
de rebotes

circle chain
cadena de círculos

checks
cuadros

repeating
repetitiva

random
al azar

overlapping
superpuesta

mirror symmetry
simetría especular

hexagonal
hexagonal

geometric patterns
patrones geométricos

stars
estrellas

polka dots
lunares

tartan
tartán

spotted
moteado

unique
único

fivefold symmetry
simetría quíntuple

hearts
corazones

radiating
radiante

simple
sencilla

complex
compleja

striped
rayado

rainbow stripes
rayas de arcoíris

Which pattern would you choose for your bedroom wallpaper?

¿Qué patrón elegirías para el papel pintado de tu cuarto?

Patterns in nature
Patrones en la naturaleza

Patterns
Patrones

Designing and making
Diseñar y fabricar

Here are words we use when we design and make things, and words for tools and machines. What would you like to make?

Aquí tienes palabras que utilizamos cuando diseñamos y fabricamos cosas, y palabras para designar herramientas y máquinas. ¿Qué te gustaría hacer?

Designing
Diseñar

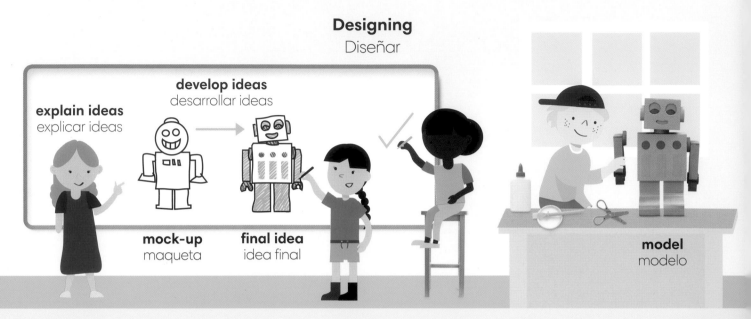

explain ideas
explicar ideas

develop ideas
desarrollar ideas

mock-up
maqueta

final idea
idea final

model
modelo

Making
Fabricar

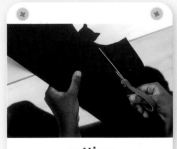

cutting
cortar

constructing
construir

shaping
dar forma

weaving
tejer

Joining
Unir

stick
encolar

tape
unir con cinta adhesiva

tie
atar

sew
coser

slot
encajar

split pin
pasador dividido

flange
pestaña

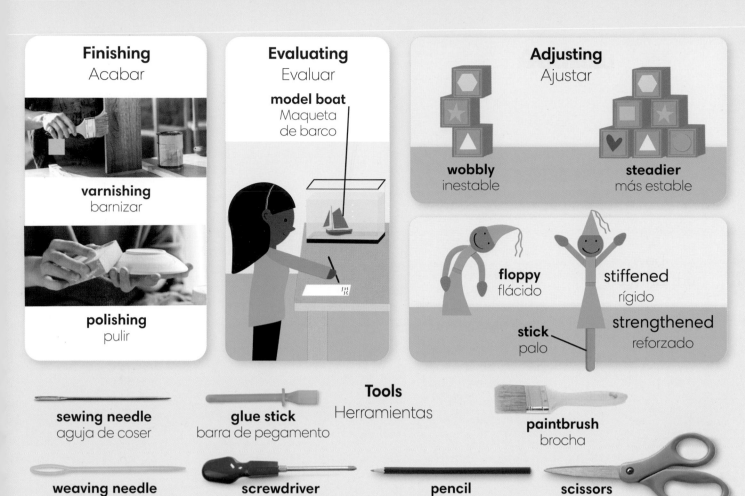

Finishing
Acabar

varnishing
barnizar

polishing
pulir

Evaluating
Evaluar

model boat
Maqueta
de barco

Adjusting
Ajustar

wobbly
inestable

steadier
más estable

floppy
flácido

stiffened
rígido

strengthened
reforzado

stick
palo

Tools
Herramientas

sewing needle
aguja de coser

glue stick
barra de pegamento

paintbrush
brocha

weaving needle
aguja de tejer

screwdriver
destornillador

pencil
lápiz

scissors
tijeras

Simple machines and technology
Máquinas simples y tecnología

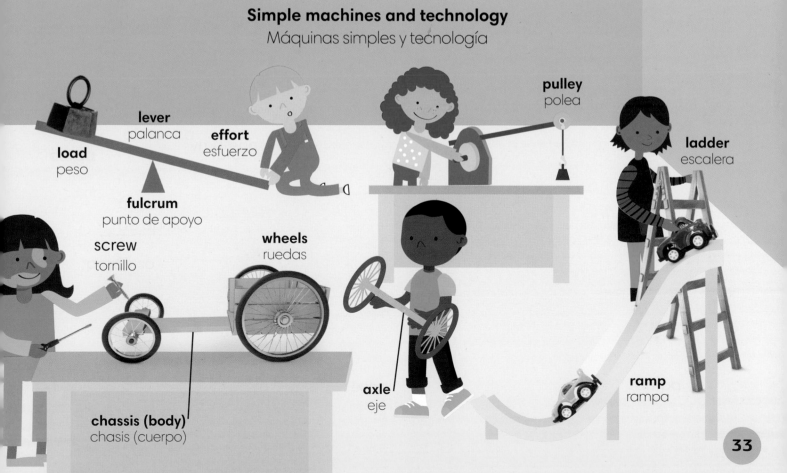

lever
palanca

effort
esfuerzo

load
peso

pulley
polea

ladder
escalera

fulcrum
punto de apoyo

screw
tornillo

wheels
ruedas

axle
eje

ramp
rampa

chassis (body)
chasis (cuerpo)

Talking about cooking
Hablar de cocinar

These words name cooking equipment and help us talk about activities we do in the kitchen.

Estas palabras nombran los utensilios de cocina y nos ayudan a hablar de las actividades que hacemos en la cocina.

What equipment might you use when making a cake?
¿Qué equipo podrías utilizar para hacer una tarta?

Preparing to cook
Prepararse para cocinar

put on an apron
ponerse un delantal

clean and dry surfaces
limpiar y secar las superficies

cleaning cloths
bayetas

Always ask an adult to help you when cooking and when using knives.
Pide siempre ayuda a un adulto para cocinar y utilizar cuchillos.

wash your hands
lavarse las manos

Kitchen utensils
Utensilios de cocina

grater
rallador

mixing bowl
bol mezclador

colander
colador

paring knife
cuchillo pequeño para verduras

carving knife
cuchillo de trinchar

carving fork
tenedor de trinchar

fish serving fork and serving knife
tenedor y cuchillo de servir pescado

Cooking
Cocinar

make cakes
hacer pasteles

cakes in a baking pan
pasteles en una bandeja de horno

wok
wok

**immersion
blender**
batidora
de mano

tongs
pinzas

spatula
espátula

ladle
cucharón

whisk
batidor

**wooden
spoon**
cuchara de
madera

pitcher
jarra

funnel
embudo

**rolling
pin**
rodillo

**cutting
board**
tabla de
cortar

**cookie
cutter**
cortador de
galletas

pot
cacerola

**pastry
brush**
pincel de
repostería

**ice-cream
scoop**
cuchara para
helado

strainer
colador

**can
opener**
abrelatas

frying pan
sartén

Cleaning up
Limpiar

**load the
dishwasher**
poner el
lavavajillas

**do the
dishes**
lavar los
platos

dish soap
jabón
lavaplatos

**spray
cleaner**
espray de
limpieza

dish sponge
estropajo

wipe surfaces
limpiar las superficies

Different foods
Distintas comidas

Here are words for some foods and the main food groups. The study of food and how it works in our bodies is called "nutrition." What's important is enjoying food and eating healthily.

Aquí tienes palabras para algunos alimentos y para los principales grupos de alimentos. El estudio de los alimentos y de cómo actúan en nuestro organismo se llama "nutrición". Lo importante es disfrutar de la comida y comer sano.

Fruits and vegetables
Frutas y verduras

pineapple
piña

fruit kebabs
brochetas de fruta

salad
ensalada

carrots
zanahorias

zucchini
calabacín

cauliflower
coliflor

eggplant
berenjena

apples
manzanas

fish
pescad

raisins
pasas

eggs
huevos

chickpeas
garbanzos

tofu
tofu

steak
filete

chicken
pollo

What fruits and vegetables would you like to eat today?
¿Qué frutas y verduras te gustaría comer hoy?

Proteins
Proteínas

Where is your food from?
¿De dónde viene lo que comes?

bread
pan

→

wheat
trigo

ginger
jengibre

→

underground stem of the ginger plant
tallo subterráneo de la planta de jengibre

blueberries
arándanos

→

blueberry plant
planta de arándanos

chocolate
chocolate

→

seeds of the cacao tree
semillas del árbol del cacao

Treats
Caprichos

fruit smoothie
batido de frutas

cookies
galletas

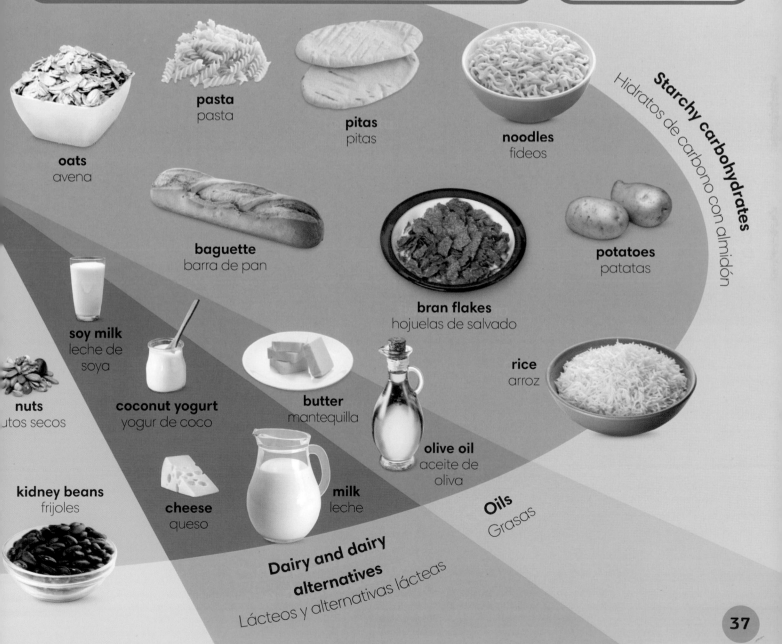

oats
avena

pasta
pasta

pitas
pitas

noodles
fideos

baguette
barra de pan

bran flakes
hojuelas de salvado

potatoes
patatas

soy milk
leche de soya

nuts
...utos secos

coconut yogurt
yogur de coco

butter
mantequilla

olive oil
aceite de oliva

rice
arroz

kidney beans
frijoles

cheese
queso

milk
leche

Starchy carbohydrates
Hidratos de carbono con almidón

Oils
Grasas

Dairy and dairy alternatives
Lácteos y alternativas lácteas

37

Know your world
Conocer el mundo

Some nouns help us to name different places on Earth, including lands and oceans. We also use nouns for the directions on a compass.

Algunos sustantivos nos ayudan a nombrar distintos lugares del planeta, como las tierras y los océanos. También utilizamos sustantivos para las direcciones de una brújula.

Rocky Mountains
montañas Rocosas

Compass
Brújula

North
norte

Northwest
noroeste

Northeast
nordeste

West
oeste

East
este

Southwest
sudoeste

Southeast
sudeste

South
South

Pacific Ocean
océano Pacífico

North America
América del Norte

Atlantic Ocean
océano Atlántico

Amazon rainforest
selva amazónica

equator
ecuador

Viewing our world
Observar nuestro mundo

Atlas

atlas
atlas

globe
globo terráqueo

Antarctic desert
desierto antártico

South America
América del Sur

Point to the part of the world you live in.

Señala la parte del mundo en la que vives.

aerial photograph
fotografía aérea

cold desert
desierto frío

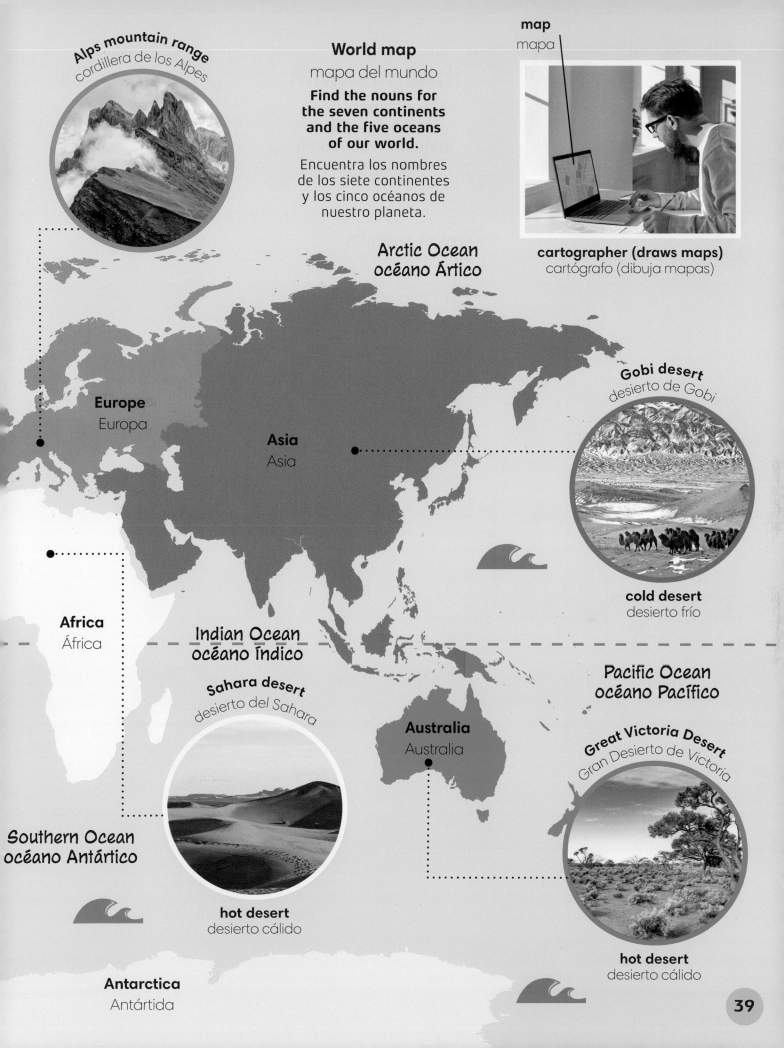

Alps mountain range
cordillera de los Alpes

World map
mapa del mundo
**Find the nouns for
the seven continents
and the five oceans
of our world.**
Encuentra los nombres
de los siete continentes
y los cinco océanos de
nuestro planeta.

map
mapa

cartographer (draws maps)
cartógrafo (dibuja mapas)

Arctic Ocean
océano Ártico

Gobi desert
desierto de Gobi

Europe
Europa

Asia
Asia

cold desert
desierto frío

Africa
África

Indian Ocean
océano Índico

Pacific Ocean
océano Pacífico

Sahara desert
desierto del Sahara

Australia
Australia

Great Victoria Desert
Gran Desierto de Victoria

Southern Ocean
océano Antártico

hot desert
desierto cálido

hot desert
desierto cálido

Antarctica
Antártida

Natural landscapes and seascapes
Paisajes naturales y marinos

These words name natural areas of the land and the ocean in our world. Some of these places are protected because they are so spectacular and unique.

Estas palabras nombran zonas naturales de la tierra y el mar en nuestro planeta. Algunos de estos lugares están protegidos porque son espectaculares y únicos.

Which of the places in these pictures would you like to visit?
¿Cuál de los lugares de estas fotos te gustaría visitar?

Land
Tierra

coast
costa

peninsula
península

mountain range
cordillera

dry canyon
cañón seco

mound
montículo

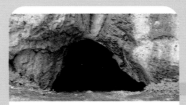

cave
cueva

lowlands
tierras bajas

highlands
tierras altas

Water
Agua

sea
mar

bay
bahía

harbor
puerto

lagoon
laguna

inlet
grao

atoll
atolón

lake
lago

river
río

stream
arroyo

river gorge
garganta de río

waterfall
cascada

glacier
glaciar

Some plant environments
Algunos entornos vegetales

forest
bosque

woodland
zona boscosa

rainforest
bosque tropical

savanna
sabana

prairie
pradera

tundra
tundra

Protected places
Lugares protegidos

Servicio de Parques Nacionales

Parque Nacional Zion

national park
parque nacional

wilderness area
espacio natural

nature reserve
reserva natural

natural monument
monumento natural

protected seascape
paisaje marino protegido

World Heritage sites
Patrimonio de la Humanidad

41

Created landscapes
Paisajes creados

Here are words for places, buildings, and other things that are created in landscapes by humans. Are you sitting in a building? What is it called?

Aquí tienes palabras para designar lugares, edificios y otras cosas creadas en los paisajes por el ser humano. ¿Estás sentado dentro de un edificio? ¿Cómo se llama?

Where we live and work
Dónde vivimos y trabajamos

village
pueblo

town
ciudad

city
ciudad

farm
granja

house
casa

cottage
bungaló

apartment building
edificio de departamentos

store
tienda

school
escuela

office
oficina

factory
fábrica

Services
Servicios

port
puerto

pier
muelle

lighthouse
faro

dam
presa

reservoir
embalse

oil rig
plataforma petrolera

transmission towers
torres eléctricas

wind farm
parque eólico

bicycle lane
carril bici

direction signs
señales de dirección

overpass
paso elevado

bridge
puente

railroad bridge
puente de ferrocarril

drain
desagüe

sewer
alcantarilla

Fun places to visit
Lugares divertidos para visitar

park
parque

adventure park
parque de aventura

water park
parque acuático

recreation center
centro recreativo

petting zoo
granja infantil

museum
museo

statue
estatua

castle ruins
castillo en ruinas

ancient wall
antigua muralla

prehistoric monument
monumento prehistórico

Long, long ago
Hace mucho tiempo

We name large groups of people from long ago "ancient civilizations." They existed thousands of years ago. Here are some ancient civilizations. Objects from the past help us learn about them.

Llamamos "civilizaciones antiguas" a grandes grupos de personas que vivieron hace mucho tiempo, hace miles de años. Estas son algunas civilizaciones antiguas. Los objetos del pasado nos ayudan a conocerlas.

Find some words that mean ruler or monarch.

Busca palabras que signifiquen gobernante o monarca.

Ancient Egypt
Antiguo Egipto

pyramids
pirámides

pharaoh
faraón

makeup
maquillaje

papyrus
papiro

hieroglyphs
jeroglíficos

Ancient China
Antigua China

imperial palace
palacio imperial

scroll
rollo

emperor
emperador

empress
emperatriz

calligraphy
caligrafía

magnetic compass
brújula magnética

Mesoamerica
Mesoamérica

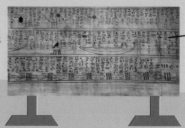

temple
templo

Mayans
mayas

Mayan calendar system
sistema de calendario maya

Mayan headdress
tocado maya

lord
señor

lady
dama

Ancient Rome
Antigua Roma

aqueduct
acueducto

emperor
emperador

empress
emperatriz

Romans
romanos

gladiator
gladiador

Roman road
calzada romana

The Ghana Empire
Imperio de Ghana

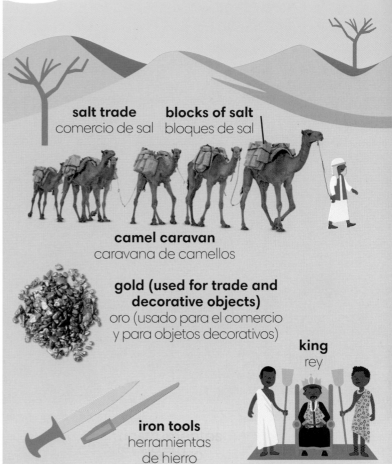

salt trade
comercio de sal

blocks of salt
bloques de sal

camel caravan
caravana de camellos

gold (used for trade and decorative objects)
oro (usado para el comercio y para objetos decorativos)

king
rey

iron tools
herramientas de hierro

Ancient Greece
Antigua Grecia

ancient Olympic Games
antiguos Juegos Olímpicos

philosopher
filósofo

king
rey

ruler
gobernante

actors
actores

theater
teatro

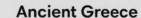

discus throwing
lanzamiento de disco

chariot racing
carreras de carros

Transportation over time
El transporte en el tiempo

Like other things, transportation has changed over time. Let's discover words for types of transportation through the ages. Which of these would you like to try?

Como otras cosas, el transporte ha cambiado con el tiempo. Descubramos palabras con las que designar tipos de transporte a lo largo de la historia. ¿Cuál te gustaría probar?

Air
Aire

hot-air balloon
globo aerostático

airship
dirigible

first powered airplane
primer avión propulsado

Water
Agua

dugout (hollowed log boat)
cayuco (barco de tronco hueco)

galleon
galeón

horse-drawn barge
barcaza tirada
por caballos

Land
Tierra

walking
caminar

horseback riding
montar a caballo

camel riding
montar a camello

**ancient
Roman chariot**
antiguo carro romano

e-bikes for rent
bicicletas eléctricas de alquiler

hybrid car
coche híbrido

high-speed train
tren de gran velocidad

**space tourism
rocket plane**
cohete avión de
turismo espacial

space shuttle
transbordador
espacial

**Apollo 11
spacecraft**
nave Apolo 11

**Saturn V
rocket**
cohete
Saturno V

Space
Espacio

**passenger
transport helicopter**
helicóptero de transporte
de pasajeros

jet airliner
avión de reacción

steamboat
barco de vapor

car ferry
ferri de automóviles

water-bus
lancha colectiva

modern cruise ship
crucero moderno

sedan chair
silla de manos

Victorian handcart
carro de mano victoriano

covered wagon
carro cubierto

steam locomotive
locomotora de vapor

electric bus
autobús eléctrico

electric tram
tranvía eléctrico

**high
wheeler**
biciclo

omnibus
omnibús

Digital communication
Comunicación digital

Here are words we use to talk about gadgets, computers, and sending information electronically. What digital devices have you used?

Estas son las palabras que utilizamos para hablar de aparatos, computadoras y envío de información por vía electrónica. ¿Qué dispositivos digitales has utilizado?

Digital devices
Dispositivos digitales

tablet
tableta

smartphone
teléfono inteligente

digital camera
cámara digital

wireless earbuds
auriculares inalámbricos

laptop
computadora portátil

microphone
micrófono

gaming headset
auriculares para juegos

gaming console and gaming controller
consola y mando de juegos

television
televisor

screen, processor, memory, and hard drive
pantalla, procesador, memoria y disco duro

webcam
cámara web

interactive whiteboard
pizarra interactiva

mouse
ratón

desktop personal computer
computadora personal de escritorio

keyboard
teclado

printer
impresora

We need to be very careful when using digital devices so that we keep ourselves and our information safe. Ask a trusted adult to help you with this.

Debemos utilizar los dispositivos digitales con mucho cuidado para mantener nuestra seguridad y la de nuestra información. Pide ayuda a un adulto de confianza.

Communication and computer symbols
Símbolos de comunicación y computadoras

log on
conexión

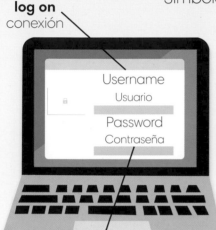

Username
Usuario

Password
Contraseña

personal information
información personal

privacy
privacidad

security
seguridad

satellite
satélite

 Wi-Fi
wifi

 document
documento

 compose
redactar

 attachment
adjunto

text
texto

avatar
avatar

Hey, how are you?
Hola, ¿cómo estás?

I'm fine, thanks!
¡Bien, gracias!

messaging
mensajería

 email
correo electrónico

chatbot (a computer program that replies to messages)
chatbot (programa informático que responde a mensajes)

friends
amigos

chat
chat

sharing
compartir

apps
app

social media
redes sociales

video call
videollamada

Creating and presenting
Crear y presentar

Let's look at words we use when we collect information, create something from information, and share information with others.

Veamos las palabras que utilizamos al recopilar información, crear algo a partir de la información y compartir información con otros.

Finding information
Encontrar información

web browser
navegador web

**URL (Uniform Resource Locator)
also known as web address**
URL (localizador uniforme de recursos)
también se denomina dirección web

reading and researching
leer e investigar

asking questions
hacer preguntas

visiting a library
visitar una biblioteca

visiting a museum
visitar un museo

going on a field trip
hacer una salida de campo

interviewing friends and family
entrevistar a amigos y familia

collecting
recolectar

finding pictures
buscar imágenes

Handling information
Manejar información

Leaf sizes
Tamaños de hojas

Big	Medium	Small
Grandes	Medianas	Pequeñas

sort
ordenar

Sorting fruit
Clasificar frutas

Red fruit
Frutas rojas

Berries
Bayas

Fruit that is red and a berry
Frutas que son rojas y son bayas

Venn diagram
diagrama de Venn

Which is the most popular pet?
¿Cuál es la mascota más popular?

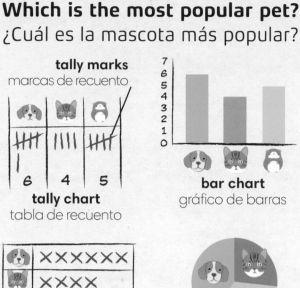

tally marks
marcas de recuento

6	4	5

tally chart
tabla de recuento

bar chart
gráfico de barras

table
tabla

pie chart
gráfico circular

Plants questionnaire
Cuestionario de plantas

Name
Nombre _____

Answer each statement by checking a face.
Contesta cada frase marcando una cara.

I agree.
Estoy de acuerdo

I disagree.
No estoy de acuerdo

	I agree. Estoy de acuerdo	I disagree. No estoy de acuerdo
I can name all parts of a plant. Sé nombrar todas las partes de una planta	😊	😞
I can name some parts of a plant Sé nombrar algunas partes de una planta	😊	😞
I can name no parts of a plant No sé nombrar ninguna parte de una planta	😊	😞

questionnaire
cuestionario

survey
encuesta

Growth of a sunflower
Crecimiento de un girasol

40 in	
32 in	
24 in	
16 in	
8 in	
0 in	

Mar Apr May Jun Jul Aug
Marzo Abril Mayo Junio Julio Agosto

graph
gráfico

Creating
Crear

drawing pictures
hacer dibujos

making notes
tomar notas

filming
filmar

How to grow a sunflower
Cómo cultivar un girasol

Presenting
Presentar

How to grow a sunflower
Cómo cultivar un girasol

poster
póster

presentation
presentación

How to grow a sunflower
Cómo cultivar un girasol

A step-by-step guide
Guía paso a paso

Slide 1
Diapositiva 1

slideshow
presentación de diapositivas

vlog
videoblog

blog
blog

live stream
transmisión en vivo

Technology innovations
Innovaciones tecnológicas

The language we use for digital toys and equipment is ever-changing. Some innovations are just for fun and games. Others help us with challenges in life.

Las palabras que utilizamos para los juguetes y los equipos digitales cambian constantemente. Algunas innovaciones son solo para entretenernos y jugar. Otras nos ayudan con las necesidades de la vida.

Which of these things would you like to use?

¿Cuál de estas cosas te gustaría utilizar?

Innovations that entertain us
Innovaciones que nos entretienen

virtual-reality headset
casco de realidad virtual

talking electronic pet
mascota electrónica parlante

virtual-reality (VR) app (makes you feel like you are in a world created by a computer)
aplicación de realidad virtual (RV) (te hace sentir como si estuvieras en un mundo creado por computadora)

touch-sensitive plasma light
luz de plasma táctil

augmented-reality (AR) app (puts 3D computer images in the real world)
aplicación de realidad aumentada (RA) (pone imágenes tridimensionales de computadora en el mundo real)

voice-changer toy
juguete que cambia la voz

Interactive projections
Proyecciones interactivas

projector
proyector

floor
suelo

wall
muro

Innovations that help us (some entertain us too!)
Innovaciones que nos ayudan (¡algunas también nos entretienen!)

e-book
libro electrónico

e-reader
lector de libros
electrónicos

smartwatch
teléfono inteligente

multitouch table
mesa multitáctil

voice assistant
asistente de voz

robotic prosthetic
prótesis robótica

**gloves that change
sign language into speech**
guantes que traducen el lenguaje
de señas en habla

**smart glasses that
read text out loud**
lentes inteligentes que
leen textos en voz alta

e-scooters
monopatín
eléctrico

e-microcar
microcoche
eléctrico

camera
cámara

quadcopter drone
dron cuadricóptero

3D printer
impresora 3-D

**adaptive gaming controller
(for gamers who have a disability)**
mando de juego adaptable
(para jugadores con discapacidad)

green screen
pantalla verde

**USB microscope (for viewing
tiny images on a computer)**
microscopio USB (para ver imágenes
diminutas en una computadora)

educational robot toy
robot educativo de juguete

portable water purifier
purificador de agua portátil

neck fan
ventilador de cuello

robot waiter
robot camarero

Making music
Hacer música

We use these words when we talk and write about music. We can perform music in fun ways, solo or with others.

Utilizamos estas palabras cuando hablamos y escribimos sobre música. Podemos interpretar música de formas divertidas, solos o con otros.

sound
sonido

Body percussion
Percusión corporal

snap
chasquido

clap
palmas

stomp
pisada

pat
palmada

Performing music
Interpretar música

solo
solo

duet
dúo

choir
coro

rock band
banda de rock

orchestra
orquesta

rap group
grupo de rap

Instruments
Instrumentos

Percussion
Percusión

mallets
mazos

xylophone
xilófono

piano (percussion and strings)
piano (percusión y cuerdas)

tambourine
pandereta

steel drums
tambores metálicos

drums
tambores

Strings
Cuerdas

bow
arco

violin
violín

guitar
guitarra

> **Do you play a musical instrument? If not, which instrument would you like to play?**
>
> ¿Tocas algún instrumento? Si no, ¿qué instrumento te gustaría tocar?

Woodwind
Madera

clarinet
clarinete

flute
flauta

Brass
Metal

French horn
trompa

trumpet
trompeta

tuba
tuba

Reading music
Leer la música

musical notes
notas musicales

quarter notes
negras

eighth notes
corcheas

The speed of a piece of music (tempo)
Velocidad de una pieza musical (tempo)

adagio (slowly like a turtle's movement)
adagio (lento como el movimiento de una tortuga)

allegro (quickly like a cheetah's movement)
allegro (rápido como el movimiento de un guepardo)

Playing sports
Practicar deportes

Here are words for some sports, some skills we use in sports, and some sports equipment. Which sports do you play or like to watch?

Aquí tienes palabras para algunos deportes, habilidades que utilizamos en los deportes y equipamientos deportivos. ¿Qué deportes practicas o te gusta ver?

resilient
resistencia

balancing
equilibrio

skateboarding
patineta

athletics
atletismo

speed
velocidad

table tennis
tenis de mesa

quick reflexes
buenos reflejos

swimming
natación

floating
flotación

pickleball
pádel

teamwork
trabajo en equipo

leaping
saltar

volleyball
voleibol

wheelchair tennis
tenis en silla de ruedas

precision
precisión

soccer
futbol

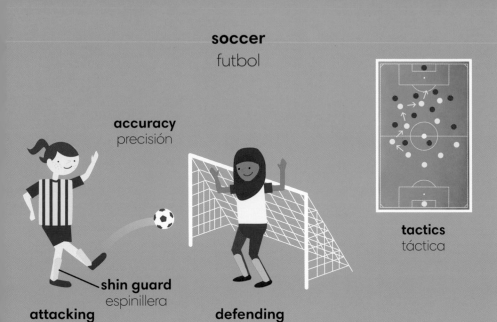

accuracy
precisión

shin guard
espinillera

attacking
atacar

defending
defender

tactics
táctica

basketball
baloncesto

shooting
lanzar

throwing
tirar

karate
karate

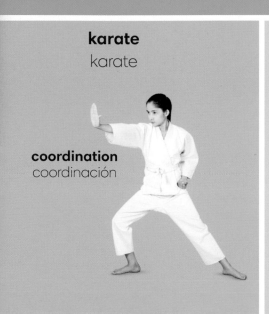

coordination
coordinación

gymnastics
gimnasia

power
potencia

baseball
béisbol

glove
guante

catching
recepción

ice hockey
hockey sobre hielo

helmet
casco

passing
pasar

endurance
resistencia

mountain biking
bicicleta de montaña

Three super sports!
¡Tres superdeportes!

Let's learn words for different kinds of athletics, gymnastics, and swimming.

Aprendamos palabras para diferentes tipos de atletismo, gimnasia y natación.

Which do you like best: running fast, swinging from bars in a playground, or splashing in a swimming pool?

¿Qué te gusta más: correr rápido, columpiarte de las barras de un parque infantil o chapotear en una piscina?

Athletics
Atletismo

Track events
Pruebas de pista

sprint
esprint

relay
relevos

long-distance running
carrera de fondo

hurdles
carrera de vallas

steeplechase
carrera de obstáculos

Field events
Pruebas de campo

Road running
Carrera en carretera

high jump
salto de altura

pole vault
salto con pértiga

long jump
salto de longitud

javelin
jabalina

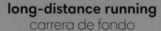

shot put
lanzamiento de peso

discus
disco

hammer
martillo

marathon
maratón

Gymnastics
Gimnasia

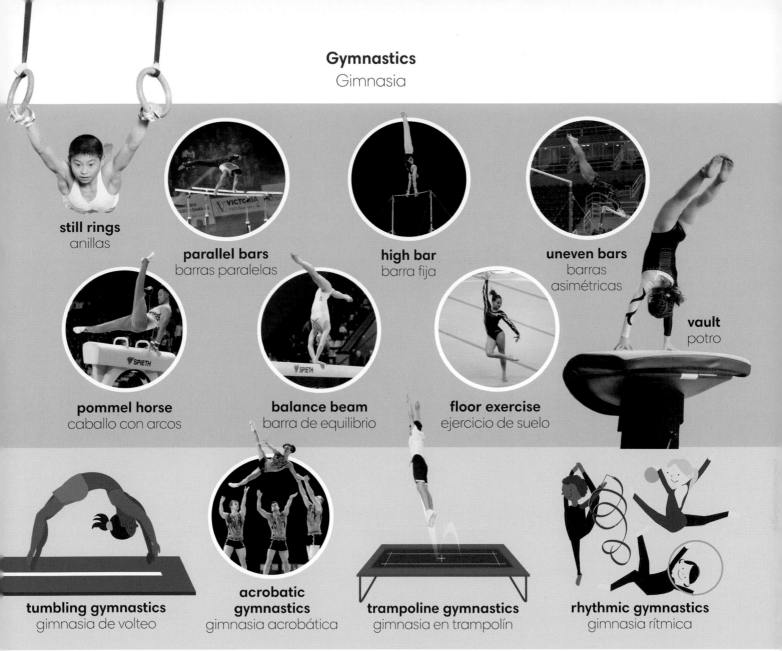

still rings
anillas

parallel bars
barras paralelas

high bar
barra fija

uneven bars
barras
asimétricas

vault
potro

pommel horse
caballo con arcos

balance beam
barra de equilibrio

floor exercise
ejercicio de suelo

tumbling gymnastics
gimnasia de volteo

**acrobatic
gymnastics**
gimnasia acrobática

trampoline gymnastics
gimnasia en trampolín

rhythmic gymnastics
gimnasia rítmica

Swimming and diving
Natación y clavados

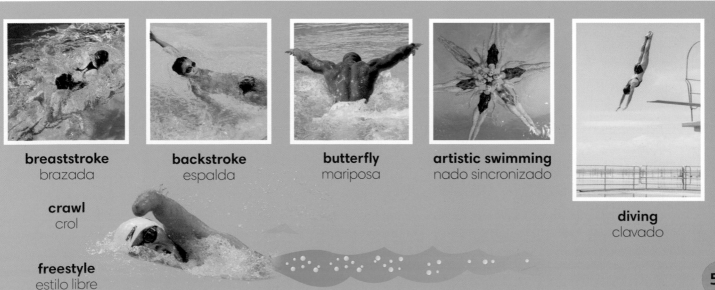

breaststroke
brazada

backstroke
espalda

butterfly
mariposa

artistic swimming
nado sincronizado

crawl
crol

diving
clavado

freestyle
estilo libre

Play and explore
Jugar y explorar

We are learning even when we are playing. Let's discover words for play areas, learning areas, and fun play equipment.

Aprendemos incluso al jugar. Descubramos las palabras de las zonas de juego y aprendizaje y de divertidos materiales de juego.

Come and write!
¡Ven a escribir!

writing area
zona de escritura

painting area
zona de pintura

Playing inside
Jugar en el interior

dress-up area
zona de disfraces

reading fort
cabaña de lectura

beanbag
puf

sensory play
juego sensorial

construction
construcción

playdough
plastilina

You can play at any age! How will you play when you are grown up?
Se puede jugar a cualquier edad. ¿Cómo jugarás cuando seas mayor?

tree swing
columpio en un árbol

parachute
paracaídas

hill to roll down
colina para bajar rodando

outdoor stage
escenario al aire libre

jungle gym
estructura para trepar

tunnel
túnel

bridge
puente

trampoline
cama elástica

seesaw
balancín

climbing net
red para trepar

slide
tobogán

light and sound play
juego de luz y sonido

Playing outside
Jugar fuera

umbrella
parasol

sand table
bandeja de arena

water table
bandeja de agua

balls
pelotas

nature area
zona natural

play cooking
jugar a cocinar

growing things
cultivar cosas

hopscotch
rayuela

stepping stones
camino de piedras

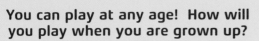

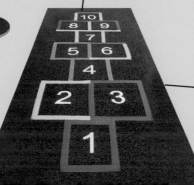
play mat
alfombra de juego

buddy bench
banco de amigos

mud kitchen
cocina de barro

Learning everywhere!
¡Aprender en todas partes!

Here are words we use to talk about school, clubs, and learning. We can learn anytime and anywhere, before, during, and after our school life.

Estas son las palabras que utilizamos para hablar de la escuela, los clubes y el aprendizaje. Podemos aprender en cualquier momento y lugar, antes, durante y después de nuestra vida escolar.

At school
En la escuela

class lining up
clase en fila

taking attendance
pasar lista

lesson time
hora de clase

library time
hora de biblioteca

break time
recreo

music
música

lunchtime
almuerzo

PE (physical education)
educación física

home time
hora de volver a casa

school show
festival escolar

A learning time line
Calendario de estudios

day care
puericultura

preschool
guardería

kindergarten
preescolar

Clubs
Clubes

art club
club de arte

drama club
club de teatro

tennis club
club de tenis

sailing club
club de vela

cooking club
club de cocina

Choose a club you'd like to join.

Elige un club al que te gustaría unirte.

dance club
club de baile

soccer club
club de futbol

Hello
Hola

language club
club de idiomas

nature club
club de naturaleza

ski club
club de esquí

School trips and outings
Viajes y salidas escolares

aquarium
acuario

natural history museum
museo de historia natural

art museum
museo de arte

nature park
parque natural

castle
castillo

elementary school
escuela primaria

high school
escuela secundaria

college
universidad

Acknowledgments
Agradecimientos

DK would like to thank: Dheeraj Arora for additional jacket design work; Geetam Biswas, Ridhima Sikka, Shubhdeep Kaur, Manpreet Kaur, and Samrajkumar for additional picture research work.

The publisher would like to thank the following for their kind permission to reproduce their photographs: (Key: a=above; b=below/bottom; c=center; f=far; l=left; r=right; t=top)

1 **Dreamstime.com:** Isselee (cb); Johnfoto (br). 2 **Dreamstime.com:** Maglara (bl). 3 **123RF.com:** lucyfry (cb); Rose-Marie Henriksson / rosemhenri (tl). **Dreamstime.com:** Photoeuphoria (clb). 6 **Alamy Stock Photo:** H. Mark Weidman Photography (bc); Myrleen Pearson (cla). **Depositphotos Inc:** belchonock (bl). **Dreamstime.com:** Monkey Business Images (br); Wavebreakmedia Ltd (cra); Yuri Arcurs (crb). **Getty Images / iStock:** E+ / sturti (clb). 7 **123RF.com:** microstockasia (c); nk2549 (cb/Brave). **Dreamstime.com:** Bellevue (bc/Door); Roman Milert (tc); Thammasak Chuenchom (cl); Chung Jin Mac (tr); Siew Mei Wong (cra); Vitaly Titov (crb); Yevgen Rychko (br). **Getty Images / iStock:** E+ / SDI Productions (cb); Olga Ignatova (clb); E+ / davidf (bl); Mr_Khan (bc); evgenyatamanenko (bc/Excited). 8 **Depositphotos Inc:** mstockagency (crb/Sign). **Dreamstime.com:** Elisabeth Burrell (cb/Dictionary); Krischam (clb/x2); Hryhorii Turik (cb). **Getty Images / iStock:** lleerogers (crb/Jar). **Getty Images:** PhotoAlto Agency RF Collections / Frederic Cirou (br). **Shutterstock.com:** Mister_X (crb). 9 **123RF.com:** chrupka (bc). **Depositphotos Inc:** luminastock (clb/Notepad). **Dreamstime.com:** Atman (cla/Eraser); Christophe Testi (cla); Boggy (ca/Brush); Sergii Kolesnyk (cla/Paper); Nao5970 (ca); Jose Manuel Gelpi Diaz (cla/Sharpner); Pearljamfan75 (cla/Pen); Alexandr Kornienko (cla/Table); Pictac (ca/Ruler); Thinglass (crb); Ruth Black (bl). **Shutterstock.com:** pikcha (ca/Tablet). 10 **Dreamstime.com:** Wirestock (cb/Hangul script). **Shutterstock.com:** KHARANI (Script). 11 **Alamy Stock Photo:** F1online digitale Bildagentur GmbH / f1 online (tr/mountain); Tony French (tr, tr/Man). **Dreamstime.com:** Andreykuzmin (b); Mila Gligoric (bl). **Getty Images / iStock:** hakule (cb); petekarici (tl, tc). **Shutterstock.com:** Mona Ahmed (br). 13 **Dreamstime.com:** Isselee (cb, bc). **Shutterstock.com:** arsa35 (cla). 14 **Dreamstime.com:** Torsakarin (bl/Carpet). **Getty Images / iStock:** Salmon Negro (tr). 15 **123RF.com:** Rose-Marie Henriksson / rosemhenri (br). **Dreamstime.com:** Hafiza Samsuddin (tl); Guido Vrola (bl/coke); Torsakarin (cr/Carpet); Pantila Terada (crb); Anke Van Wyk (bl/Steak). **Getty Images / iStock:** clubfoto (cla/Fruit); E+ / LauriPatterson (tr). 16 **123RF.com:** Oksana Tkachuk (crb/Flower). **Dorling Kindersley:** Stephen Oliver (cr). **Dreamstime.com:** Grafner (r/2xIce cream); Pytyczech (bl); Mikhail Kokhanchikov (bc). 17 **123RF.com:** Ekaterina Pereverzeva (r/2xMusic notes). **Dreamstime.com:** Milic Djurovic (ca/Slide); Eastmanphoto (cra/Squirrel); Svetlana Foote (tr/Bird). **Getty Images / iStock:** Antagain (bl). 18 **123RF.com:** gongzstudio (ca/Speed line). **Dreamstime.com:** Alexstar (cra/Magnifying); Saravn (cl/br); Boris Medvedev (cb/Drum); Taweesak Sriwannawit (bl). **Getty Images / iStock:** lightphoto (Background). 19 **123RF.com:** Aliaksei Hintau / viselchak (crb/Dragonfly); Eric Isselee (cla). **Dorling Kindersley:** Andy and Gill Swash (clb). **Dreamstime.com:** Michael Chatt (bc/Meadowlark); Mikelane45 (clb/Wren); Zhbampton (ca/10xBeetle); Prapass Wannapinij / Prapass (cra); Geza Farkas (cb); Isselee (crb); Mark Turner (crb/Meganeura); Sean Pavone (br/2xPond). **Getty Images / iStock:** lightphoto (bl/4xBackground). **Shutterstock.com:** Milano M (cb/Calendar); Aleksandr Pobedimskiy (cra/Sandstone, cla/2xSandstone). 20 **Shutterstock.com:** BigApple orathai hanthong (b); Mister_X (c); Mega Pixel (cr/Dice). 21 **123RF.com:** tinna2727 (cla). **Dreamstime.com:** Juan Hernandez Carmona (br/Buttons); Ennjee (tr/Poles); Studioloco (cra). **Getty Images:** Moment / Sergey Mironov (ca/Track). **Getty Images / iStock:** shapecharge (ca). **Shutterstock.com:** FamVeld (tl). 23 **Alamy Stock Photo:** Geoff du Feu (cra/Cage). **Dreamstime.com:** Roman Milert (tr). 24 **Depositphotos Inc:** stockimagefactory.com (clb). **Dreamstime.com:** Aprescindere (crb); Pavel Kobysh (cla); Elena Schweitzer / Egal (cra); Chernetskaya (cra/Red bottle); Cloki (ca/Water); Palians (c/Stopwatch); Artiom Storojenco (cr); Madamlead (cb/Beaker); Anton Starikov (cb/Jug, cb/Bowl). **Getty Images / iStock:** E+ / pinstock (cb); urfinguss (c). **Shutterstock.com:** Art_Photo (ca); Studio Romantic (bl). 25 **Depositphotos Inc:** assumption111 (br); stockimagefactory.com (cl/Boy). **Dreamstime.com:** Piotr Adamowicz (clb/Board); Tatyana Vychegzhanina (tl); Oleg Beloborodov (tl/Water); Yunkiphotoshot (tr/Girl); Vadim Zakharishchev (cl). **Shutterstock.com:** T.TATSU (cr). 26 **Dreamstime.com:** Andriy Dykun (cla); Odarka Rusanenko (cla/Scarf); Evgeny Karandaev (ca, cb/Bottle); PixMarket (cb); Anton Starikov (cl/Rocks, crb); Sirikornt (cl); Sarah2 (clb); Serg_velusceac (cb/Fabric). 27 **123RF.com:** belchonock (clb/Gloves); martyhaas (ca). **Dreamstime.com:** Vlad Ageshin (tl/Door); Nexus7 (tl); Fang Jia / Clarkfang (tc/Mirror); Audines (tc); Jiri Hera (tr); Sally Herbert (tr/Hat); Irina Tiumentseva (cla); Christophe Testi (cla/Pencil); Timages (ca/Boots); Elizabeth Cummings (cra); Luisangel70 (clb); Sharpshot (cb/Stone); George Tsartsianidis (cb); Anna Khomulo (crb); Alfio Scisetti (crb/Cactus); Ping20k (bl); LOFT39Studio (bl/Pebble); Mycolor (br/Ruler). **Shutterstock.com:** ChebanenkoAnn (br). 28 **123RF.com:** Dndavis (cla/Handprint); picsfive (6xTape). **Dorling Kindersley:** Dave King / Rotring UK Ltd (cra/Pencil). **Dreamstime.com:** MingWei Chan (cl); Hypermania37 (crb/Chalk); Alison Gibson (crb/Texture); Nui7711 (bl/Frame); Elena8888 (clb); Chotewang (bl); Dansopdedeel (bl/Painting); Tuja66 (bc); Steven Jones (br); Valpal (br/Pot). **Getty Images / iStock:** spinspinspin (c/2xTexture). 29 **Dreamstime.com:** Sergey Kolesnikov (cla/Close up, ca); Linusy (clb/Splashes). **Getty Images / iStock:** ChamilleWhite (bl); Silmen (br/Easels); Bob Vector (cra); tovovan (br). **Getty Images:** Maria Swrd (cla/2xLandscape). 30 **Dreamstime.com:** Andrey Golubtsov (cla); Hibrida13 (cr/crosshatch); Katrintimoff (cr). 31 **123RF.com:** lamika (cb/Black Dots). **Dreamstime.com:** Svitlana Borokh (cla/Diamond); Ihor Patsay (cla/Hexagon); Cienpies Design / Illustrations (cla/3d hexagon); Samolevsky (cla); arko Savic (tl); Costasz (tc); Pimmimemom (tr/Butterfly); Aleksandr Rybalko (tr); Doozydo (ca/Stars); Witchera (ca); Serkorkin (cb); Rebius (cra/Cheetah); Lukas Jonaitis (cra); Maria Castellanos (cra/Flower); Vectorsoul (clb); Gabriel Robledo (crb/Zebra). **Getty Images / iStock:** DigitalVision Vectors / ulimi (clb/Hearts). **Shutterstock.com:** PongMoji (crb). 32 **Dorling Kindersley:** Dave King / Jemma Westing (cra). **Dreamstime.com:** Ansis (crb); Lightfieldstudiosprod (clb/Cutting); Mariia Symchych Navrotska (clb); Jinaritt Thongruay (crb/Weaving). **Getty Images / iStock:** UroshPetrovic (cra/Robot). **Shutterstock.com:** Hilch (cla). 33 **123RF.com:** Milic Djurovic (crb/Ladder). **Dreamstime.com:** Jaroslaw Grudzinski / jarek78 (clb/Screw); Victor Savushkin (ca/Needle); Dmitry Marchenko (cla); Alfio Scisetti (cra). **Shutterstock.com:** 3Dalia (clb); Hayran1 (cl); Olezzo (tl). 34 **Dreamstime.com:** Luisa Vallon Fumi (cr); Melica (ca); Anton Starikov (ca/Bowl); Wolna (cra); Bohuslav Jelen (c/x2). **Getty Images / iStock:** Garrett Aitken (clb); Baloncici (clb/Green towel). 35 **123RF.com:** lucyfry (ca/Star). **Dreamstime.com:** Blackslide (tl/Wok); VectorHome (tl); Gavran333 (tc/Tongs, ca/Board); Eric Simard (tc); Maglara (cla); Viacheslav Krisanov (ca); Nikolai Sorokin (cra); Desiga (cl); Littleman (clb); Thomas Gowanlock (cr); Dio5050 (br). 36 **Dreamstime.com:** Andersastphoto (clb/Cauliflower); Fortyforks (cra); Johnfoto (cra/Salad); Hyrman (cl); Jaroslaw Grudzinski (c); Rimglow (cb); Kkovaleva (cb/Apples); Edward Westmacott (crb/Fish); Anita Kumari (crb); Atman (cb/Eggs); Kaiskynet (clb); Santusya (bc); Ulga (cb/Steak); Marazem (br/Chicken). 37 **123RF.com:** natika (tc/Ginger). **Depositphotos Inc:** serezniy (clb/Yogurt). **Dreamstime.com:** Artjazz (cra/cacao); Prostockstudio (bl); Ovydyborets (clb); Szemeno (tl); Margo555 (tl/Wheat); Anat Chantrakool (tc, cb); Nevinates (clb/Nuts, cla, crb); Voltan1 (cla/Plant); Gresei (ca); Donna Marie Vincent (cla/Oats); Iaroshenkomarina (cla/Pasta); Max Lashcheuski (cra/Noodles); Puripat Khummungkhoon (clb/Milk); Valentyn75 (cb/Oil); Oriori (bc/Jug). **Getty Images / iStock:** E+ / ma-k (tr); subodhsathe (crb/Rice). **Shutterstock.com:** Suradech Prapairat (cra). 38 **Dreamstime.com:** Photoeuphoria (clb); Mariusz Prusaczyk (cb); Aleh Varanishcha (bl); Staphy (bc); Teresa Virbickis (tr). **Getty Images / iStock:** Denis Lytiagin (cla). 39 **Dreamstime.com:** Elenatur (tl); Lacheev (tr); Simone Matteo Giuseppe Manzoni (bl). **Getty Images / iStock:** Photo Italia LLC (br). **Getty Images:** Stone / Timothy Allen (cr). 40 **Alamy Stock Photo:** aerial-photos.com (cb). **Dreamstime.com:** Karen Appleyard (crb/Highlands); Neurobite (cl/coast); Minnystock (cr); Boris Panasyuk (clb); Artur Jakubowski (clb/Cave); Marcello Celli (crb); Iofoto (crb/Inlet); Fabio Lamanna (crb/Atoll); Denys Bilytskyi (cb/Lagoon); Pablo Caridad (br/Glacier); Biletskiy (br); Vogelsp (bc); Mrsixinthemix (bc/Stream); Marek Uliasz (bl); Wirestock (bl/Lake). **Getty Images / iStock:** Aekkarat Doungmaneerattana (clb/Bay); Anne Lindgren (cr/Canyon); frederikloewer (clb/Ocean). **Getty Images:** Moment / carlo alberto conti (cl). 41 **Alamy Stock Photo:** Dennis Frates (ca); Richard Green (br/Canyon); Ingo Oeland (br). **Dreamstime.com:** Chris Boswell (clb); Karsten Neglia (tl); Gleb Ivanov (tr); Maciej Czekajewski (cla); Premekm (cra); Vitaly Titov (bl). **Getty Images / iStock:** Fabian Gysel (crb). **Getty Images:** The Image Bank / James Warwick (crb/Nature). **Shutterstock.com:** Ely C (bc). 42 **123RF.com:** Vladimir Yudin / rrraven (t). **Dreamstime.com:** Haizul (crb/Apartment); Macrovector (br). **Shutterstock.com:** Tupungato (cl/Housesx3). 43 **123RF.com:** Dimitar Marinov / oorka (ca). **Dreamstime.com:** Steve Allen (bl); Vicente Rubio (tc); Trondur (cla); Chris Hamilton / Chimpey (cla/Electricity); Cbechinie (cra/Cyclist); Timrobertsaerial (cl); Erix2005 (c); Valentina Moraru (cr); Mulderphoto (cr/Sewer); Olena Korol (clb); Peter Etchells (cb); Wing Ho Tsang (crb); Mineria6 (crb/Farm); Andreadonetti (bl/Statue); Physiodave (bc); Caoerlei (br/Wall); Jblackstock (br). **Getty Images / iStock:** bluejayphoto (cl/Bridge); Sean Pavone (tr/Dam). **Getty Images:** Westend61 (tl). **Shutterstock.com:** Anita van den Broek (tl/Port); Rita Image (cra); John_T (clb/Park). 44 **Alamy Stock Photo:** Christine Osborne Pictures (cla/pharaoh); Prawns (br); GRANGER - Historical Picture Archive (bc); Science History Images (bc/Compass); CPA Media Pte Ltd (cb/Empress); ICP / incamerastock (cb); Imaginechina Limited (clb). **Dreamstime.com:** Andreykuzmin (bl/Scroll); Tiago Lopes Fernandez (crb); Tanya Borozenets (cla); Edwardgerges (cr); Kateryna Kolesnyk (cra). **Getty Images / iStock:** Bjdlzx (bl). 45 **Alamy Stock Photo:** Vito Arcomano (cl); Lebrecht Music & Arts (bl); The Picture Art Collection (clb); Juergen Schonnop (tl); Erin Babnik (cla); FOST (cla/Empress). **Bridgeman Images:** © NPL - DeA Picture Library (cb). **Dreamstime.com:** Gillespaire (ca); Kvasay (br, crb); Therina Groenewald (cra). **Shutterstock.com:** Sanit Fuangnakhon (cl/Roman statue). 46 **Alamy Stock Photo:** Lebrecht Music & Arts (cla); North Wind Picture Archives (c); De Luan (cra). **Dorling Kindersley:** Egle Kazdailyte (crb). **Dreamstime.com:** Corners74 (bl); Kalman89 (br); Dreammediapeel (bc); Darren Curzon (cr). **Shutterstock.com:** Everett Collection (ca). 47 **Alamy Stock Photo:** Everett Collection Inc / Ron Harvey (crb/Covered Frontier); Glasshouse Images / JT Vintage (clb); Montagu Images / Laurence Heyworth (clb/Sedan Chair); Pictorial Press Ltd (br, cl); PA Images (cla). **Dreamstime.com:** Abdellah Amed (cra/Smoke); Wisconsinart (br/High Wheel Bicycle); Simas2 (bl); Irinabal18 (bl/Electrobus); Hasan Zaidi (cr); Baloncici (cr/Clipper); Boarding1now (cla/Airplane); Bjrn Wylezich (cl/ferry). **Getty Images:** AFP / Patrick T. Fallon (tl). **NASA:** (cra, tc). **Shutterstock.com:** Arcansel (crb). 48 **123RF.com:** Piotr Adamowicz (crb); George Mdivanian (crb/TV). **Dreamstime.com:** Axstokes (cla); Monkey Business Images (br); Chernetskaya (bc); Kenishirotie (bl); Liouthe (ca). **Shutterstock.com:** GreenLandStudio (cla/Tablet); Dmytro_Kryzhanovskyi (cb); Third of november (clb); LuxMockup (cra). 49 **Dreamstime.com:** Axstokes (bl, crb); Prostockstudio (br); Rawf88 (cb); Vladimir Timofeev (cra). **Getty Images / iStock:** AsiaVision (bc). 50 **123RF.com:** Greek / Sergey Kolesov (ca). **Depositphotos Inc:** monkeybusiness (br). **Dreamstime.com:** Dragonimages (cra); Wavebreakmedia Ltd (cb); Rmarmion (clb/Library); Photographerlondon (crb/Field Trip); Meolia (bc). **Shutterstock.com:** NataliyaBack (crb). 51 **123RF.com:** Greek / Sergey Kolesov (bc). **Dreamstime.com:** Diego Vito Cervo (br); Ssstocker (b/X3); Scyther5 (br/Laptop); Chernetskaya (br/Singing); Nerss (cla). **Getty Images / iStock:** Bullet_Chained (tc); DragonFly (cla/Watermelon); spinspinspin (t/X5). 52 **123RF.com:** Smuay (cr). **Alamy Stock Photo:** Aleksei Gorodenkov (bc). **Dreamstime.com:** Ekaterina Morozova (cl); Ventura69 (br). **Getty Images:** Corbis News / Horacio Villalobos (crb). **Shutterstock.com:** Muhammah Haseeb (clb); Pixel-Shot (bl); Wavebreakmedia (c). 53 **Alamy Stock Photo:** IMAGO / Peng Lijun / Xinhua / Joseph Mizere (ca); Douglas Scott (br/Food Server); PA Images / Anthony Devlin (clb); Peter Noyce GEN (tl); Keith Morris (tr). **Depositphotos Inc:** Gorodenkoff (clb); lucadp (tl/Smartwatch). **Dreamstime.com:** Allagreeg (bl/Robot); Sylvain Robin (cl); Dmitry Marchenko (cl/Car); Nikolay Antonov (cr); Info849943 (tr/Voice Assistant). **Getty Images:** Anadolu (cla). **Getty Images / iStock:** E+ / Olemedia (cra). **Science Photo Library:** Cordelia Molloy (bl). **Shutterstock.com:** Maryshot (cr/3D printer); Liu Yangjun (br); Fabio Oliveira 2020 (crb). 54 **Dreamstime.com:** Aaron Amat (cla); Monkey Business Images (crb); Richard Gunion (cra). **Getty Images / iStock:** E+ / Sturti (clb). **Shutterstock.com:** Naluwan (ca); ViDI Studio (cla/Solo). 55 **Alamy Stock Photo:** Travelshots.com / Peter Phipp (tr). **Depositphotos Inc:** Ahavelaar (tr/Drum kit). **Dreamstime.com:** Ababaka (cla/Violin); Wiseantwork (bl); Denys Kovtun (cb); Tarasenko Maksym (crb); Wave Break Media Ltd (cr); Xavier Gallego Morell (cra); Woraphon Banchobdi (cla); Prathan Nakdontree (tl); Rolmat (tl/Piano); Thomas Perkins (tc); Lunja87 (tr/Drums). **Getty Images:** The Image Bank / Peter Dazeley (clb). 56 **Dreamstime.com:** Volodymyr Melnyk (bc). **Getty Images:** Photodisc / Sot (br). **Shutterstock.com:** Diignat (bl). 57 **123RF.com:** Kostiantyn Kuznetsov (br). **Alamy Stock Photo:** Tetra Images / Chris Grill (tr/Girl); Visuals Stock (cl). **Dreamstime.com:** Convisum (tc); Steven Day (cr); Dmitriy Melnikov (bl). **Shutterstock.com:** Onur Ozgen (tr). 58 **123RF.com:** Spotpoint74 (cl). **Alamy Stock Photo:** Cultura Creative RF / Roberto Peri (cb). **Dreamstime.com:** Auris (b/Grass); Sandra Manske (bc); Sports Photos (clb); Denys Kuvaiev (clb/Pole vault); Michael Turner (crb); Leong Chee Onn (crb/Marathon); Serrnovik (cl/Baton Runs); MaxiSports (c); Darko Cvetanoski (cr). **Getty Images / iStock:** E+ / SolStock (bc/Discus); Nosyrevy (ca). **Shutterstock.com:** WoodysPhotos (cr/huddle). 59 **Depositphotos Inc:** PantherMediaSeller (cb). **Dreamstime.com:** Ammentorp (crb); Petesaloutos (crb/Artistic swimming); Renato Borlaza (clb); Aleksandr Makarenko (c); Sasha Samardzija (cra); Photosvit (ca); Michele Morrone (cla); Stoyo Petkov (tl); Zhukovsky (tr). **Getty Images:** AFP / Dirk Waem (cl). **Getty Images / iStock:** DigitalVision / Image Source (tl/still rings). **Shutterstock.com:** Alex Bogatyrev (tc); Hairul_Nizam (bl); Quintanilla (clb/Breaststroke); ID1974 (ca/Floor Exercise). 60 **123RF.com:** Jehsomwang (cb/Pirate hat). **Depositphotos Inc:** DenysKuvaiev (bl). **Dreamstime.com:** Creativesunday (crb); Monkey Business Images (br); Panitan Kanchanwong (br); Mirela Schenk (cb). 61 **Dreamstime.com:** James Granger (br); Oksix (tr); Nagy-bagoly Ilona (cra); Dmitry Rogatnev (ca); Denis Pepin (cb); Sergeyoch (cb/Tennis Ball); Martin Mullen (bl). 62 **Dreamstime.com:** Chernetskaya (clb/lunchtime); Iftachul Farida (tr); Monkey Business Images (cla/registration, ca, bc, br); Wavebreakmedia Ltd (cr); Rido (cra/Break time, crb); Wiseantwork (clb); Konstantin Shishkin (cb); Anton Petrychenko (crb/school show). **Getty Images / iStock:** E+ / Lostinbids (bl). **Shutterstock.com:** Image Source Trading Ltd (cla). 63 **Alamy Stock Photo:** Justin Kase z12z (crb/Castle). **Dreamstime.com:** Digoarpi (tr/PALAMOS); Anna Tolipova (tr); Poznyakov (tl/Children); Iakov Filimonov (cla); Weedezign (ca); Monkey Business Images (cra, crb, bl, bl/secondary, bc, bc/colleges); Petr Zamecnik (clb); Seventyfourimages (cb); Hongqi Zhang (aka Michael Zhang) (br). **Getty Images / iStock:** E+ / Phynart Studio (tl); E+ / Pixdeluxe (tr); FatCamera (cla/Soccer). 64 **Dreamstime.com:** Prapass Wannapinij / Prapass (tr)

Cover images: *Front:* **123RF.com:** belchonock cb/ (Gloves), lucyfry crb/ (Star), Rose-Marie Henriksson / rosemhenri cla; **Dreamstime.com:** Andreykuzmin bc, Axstokes clb/ (phone), MingWei Chan tl/ (Foot), Jose Manuel Gelpi Diaz tr, Elena Schweitzer / Egal cb, Geza Farkas bl/ (Bird), Gillespaire tc, Grafner bl/ (Ice cream), Hyrman tc/ (Carrots), Isselee crb, tl/ (Bird), Birgit Korber cb/ (Bunny), Konstantin Kirillov / Kvkirillov clb, Maglara bc/ (Jug), Nevinates clb/ (Blueberries), Photoeuphoria crb/ (Globe), Rimglow clb/ (Eggplant), Valpal crb/ (Pot), Guido Vrola br, Zhbampton clb/ (Beetle); **Getty Images / iStock:** Antagain clb/ (Butterfly), Bjdlzx bc/ (Calligraphy), Salmon Negro crb/ (Plates); **NASA:** tl; *Back:* **123RF.com:** belchonock tr/ (Gloves), lucyfry cla/ (Star), Rose-Marie Henriksson / rosemhenri clb; **Dreamstime.com:** Andreykuzmin ca/ (Scroll), Jose Manuel Gelpi Diaz crb, Geza Farkas ca, Gillespaire br/ (Gold), Grafner clb/ (Ice cream), Hyrman crb/ (carrots), Isselee tl, Birgit Korber tr, Konstantin Kirillov / Kvkirillov tl/ (Pan), Maglara cr, Nevinates tc, Photoeuphoria tl/ (Globe), Rimglow tc/ (Eggplant), Valpal bl/ (Pot), Guido Vrola cla; **Getty Images / iStock:** Antagain bc/ (Butterfly), Bjdlzx ca/ (Calligraphy); **NASA:** cl; *Spine:* **Dreamstime.com:** MingWei Chan b, Birgit Korber cb/ (Bunny), Photoeuphoria t; **Getty Images / iStock:** Antagain ca